Original title:
Feelings Danced in Daydreams

Copyright © 2024 Creative Arts Management OÜ
All rights reserved.

Author: Ryan Sterling
ISBN HARDBACK: 978-9916-90-638-5
ISBN PAPERBACK: 978-9916-90-639-2

Whispers of a Wandering Heart

In the stillness of the night,
A heart drifts like a feather,
Carried by dreams untold,
Searching for a tether.

Beneath the stars so bright,
Voices whisper softly,
Tales of places unseen,
Moments spent at lofty.

Each step a gentle sigh,
In fields of endless blue,
The world spins softly by,
In search of something true.

With every fleeting glance,
A story starts to weave,
In the dance of chance and fate,
The heart learns how to believe.

Echoes of Hidden Longing

In shadows where dreams linger,
Yearnings find their way,
A faint yet constant whisper,
Echoes of yesterday.

Through the veil of silence,
A song begins to rise,
Notes of love unspoken,
Caught in unbound skies.

Each echo tells a tale,
Of wishes made in vain,
Yet still they softly call,
Through joy and through the pain.

Beneath the moon's soft light,
A heart begins to see,
That hidden in the dark,
Is the spark of destiny.

Shadows of a Sunlit Reverie

In the warmth of golden rays,
Shadows stretch and play,
Whispers of forgotten dreams,
Drift gently, fade away.

Dancing through the meadow,
Hearts weave tales of yore,
Every step a story,
That yearns to be explored.

Cascades of laughter echo,
Amongst the brightening scene,
In the corners of the mind,
Lies the magic still unseen.

As daylight turns to dusk,
Reflections fill the air,
In shadows of a reverie,
Lives a love beyond compare.

Chasing the Mirage of Tomorrow

In the desert of desire,
Dreams shimmer like the sun,
Chasing mirages in the sand,
The journey's just begun.

Through the haze of hopes and fears,
A figure starts to rise,
Guided by the light ahead,
With courage in their eyes.

Each step a whispered promise,
Written in the stars,
A dance of fate and fortune,
That mends all of the scars.

Though the road is winding,
And moments often slow,
Chasing the mirage of tomorrow,
Is where true wanderers glow.

Whispered Wishes in an Infinite Sky

In the silence of the night,
Stars dance with dreams so bright.
Each whisper carries a hope,
Floating gently, learning to cope.

Beneath the vast, eternal dome,
Hearts find solace, they roam.
Silent wishes kissed by light,
Guide the lost through the night.

Threads of Light Weaving into Tomorrow

A tapestry of bright visions,
Threads connecting our decisions.
Each stitch a moment, vivid and true,
Weaving paths that lead to you.

Upon the loom of endless time,
Patterns emerge, rhythm, and rhyme.
Guiding souls through shared intent,
Binding us with love's cement.

The Quiet Pulse of Unraveled Thoughts

In the stillness, whispers collide,
Dancing lightly as they glide.
Thoughts unraveling, a soft embrace,
Finding peace in the quiet space.

Echoes of dreams linger on,
As dawn breaks and shadows are gone.
With every heartbeat, truth is sought,
In the silence, wisdom is wrought.

Horizons of Emotions Under a Painted Sky

Colors burst in evening's glow,
Emotions rise, ebb, and flow.
The horizon blushes with unspoken fears,
A canvas painted with laughter and tears.

Underneath the expansive view,
Hearts entwined in shades anew.
Each sunset whispers a tale untold,
A beautiful journey through colors bold.

Beyond the Veil of the Ordinary

In shadows deep, where whispers dwell,
The ordinary fades, a magic spell.
Each glance reveals a hidden grace,
Life's tapestry, a wondrous space.

With colors bright, and dreams so bold,
A world unfolds, a story told.
Beyond the veil, where visions play,
Awakening wonders in disarray.

In every breath, a chance to see,
The beauty in our mystery.
Through hidden paths, we'll wander free,
Embracing all that we can be.

Sculpture of Thought in the Gallery of Night

In shadows soft, the thoughts take flight,
Carved in dreams, the sculpted night.
Whispers echo through silent halls,
A gallery where the starlight calls.

Each moment captured, a timeless piece,
In still reflections, we find our peace.
Glimmering dreams, like stars they gleam,
A canvas painted from the heart's dream.

In this exhibit of hidden grace,
We wander through the vast embrace.
As sculptures breathe and shadows sigh,
The night unfolds, we learn to fly.

Emotions Swaying to a Celestial Beat

In cosmic rhythms, feelings rise,
A dance unfolds beneath the skies.
With every pulse, our hearts align,
To the melody of the divine.

Emotions sway like leaves in air,
A symphony of love and care.
As stars create a glowing path,
We learn to cherish joy and wrath.

In gentle waves, our spirits flow,
Sculpted by the winds that blow.
Together we create a song,
In cosmic beats, where we belong.

The Unseen Waltz of Daylight Hues

In morning's glow, the colors blend,
A waltz of light that tools transcend.
Soft pastels dance, then bold and bright,
The unseen rhythm of pure delight.

With every shade, the world awakes,
As daylight weaves through every break.
A tapestry of hues unfolds,
In nature's arms, a story told.

The painted sky, a gentle sigh,
Beneath its gaze, the dreams can fly.
In moments lost, we find the muse,
In daylight's waltz, we can't refuse.

Serendipity's Silken Embrace

In a world where paths entwine,
Fortune smiles, a gentle sign.
Whispers dance on evening's air,
Life's sweet gifts found everywhere.

Moments pause, they softly play,
Turning night into bright day.
Chance encounters weave a thread,
In every heart, adventure spreads.

Unseen roads lead us to grace,
Every glance, a warm embrace.
Unfolding dreams, so tenderly,
In serendipity's decree.

With every step we dare to take,
Woven futures come awake.
In life's quilt, each stitch a chance,
We find our joy in happenstance.

Mirthful Secrets Beneath Starlit Skies

Underneath the twinkling dome,
Laughter calls, inviting home.
Secrets whispered from the night,
Shadows dance in silver light.

Every star a story's cue,
A memory cherished anew.
Hearts unite in shared delight,
Wishes born from purest sight.

Moonbeams play on sleepy streams,
Crafting tales from fading dreams.
In the stillness, joy takes flight,
Mirthful hearts with boundless sight.

Together we weave our lore,
Beneath the vast celestial floor.
Hand in hand, we chase the glow,
In the embrace of night's warm flow.

The Ballet of Forgotten Wishes

In shadows where lost hopes reside,
The ballet of dreams, cast aside.
Silhouettes of what once could be,
Twirl softly in a memory.

Each pirouette, a whispered prayer,
For chances missed, a lover's stare.
Yearning spirits grace the floor,
In the silence, we crave more.

With every leap, a gust of fate,
Wishes spinning, never late.
Bound by time's relentless chase,
Lost desires find their place.

A final bow, a tender grace,
Forgotten wishes, we embrace.
In the echo of their song,
We remember where we belong.

Colors Blurring on an Aerial Canvas

Brushstrokes mingle in the sky,
Crimson waves drift gently by.
Each hue tells a vibrant tale,
As day whispers, night sails.

Clouds become like paints in flight,
Splashing dreams in soft twilight.
An artist's heart, unleashed in flow,
Creates a world where emotions grow.

From azure blue to golden sheen,
Worlds collide where we have been.
Nature's palette, wide and free,
Crafts horizons for us to see.

Colors fading, merging fast,
Moments cherished, never last.
On this canvas, life's embrace,
A breathtaking, fleeting space.

Echoes of a Wandering Heart

In the quiet night, whispers call,
Footprints linger, shadows fall.
A restless spirit roams the land,
Dreams like grains of golden sand.

Under starlit skies, paths entwine,
Each heart's echo, a tale divine.
With every step, the journey starts,
Tracing the map of wandering hearts.

Starlit Reflections Under a Shimmering Sky

Beneath the veil of twilight glow,
Stars alight, a celestial show.
Dreams dance softly on the breeze,
Whispers of night, a gentle tease.

Reflections shimmer on the lake,
In every ripple, memories wake.
Each twinkle speaks of love so deep,
Guarding secrets that night will keep.

Fantasies Unfolding in Gentle Breezes

In gardens where the wildflowers play,
Fantasies frolic, come what may.
Colors bloom in every hue,
Whispers of magic, old yet new.

Butterflies drift through sunlit air,
Carrying wishes, sweet and rare.
In gentle breezes, dreams ignite,
Cradled softly in the light.

Chasing Shadows in the Light of Hope

Footsteps echo on a winding road,
Carrying dreams with every load.
Through the shadows, light will gleam,
Chasing fears, unfurling dreams.

Hope's warm glow, a guiding star,
Leading us near, no matter how far.
In each moment, a chance to cope,
Finding strength in the light of hope.

Aurora of Sentiments in a Cosmic Dance

Beneath the skies, colors unfurl,
Heartbeats rise, in a twirling swirl,
Stars whisper dreams, in vibrant hues,
Cosmic ballet, where hope renews.

Eclipsing shadows, twilight's embrace,
Fleeting moments, time can't erase,
Echoes of laughter, the night so bright,
In every pulse, a flicker of light.

Galaxies spin, in unison play,
Dancing with souls, night turns to day,
Each gentle brush, fate's tender hand,
Crafting a world, where sorrows disband.

Infinite journeys, through space we glide,
In the auroras, our dreams reside,
A tapestry woven, both near and far,
In this cosmic dance, we are who we are.

Shadows of Anchored Dreams on the Horizon

In the dusk, shadowed whispers sigh,
Memories linger, like birds in the sky,
Beneath the stars, lost hopes reside,
Anchored in dreams, where dreams confide.

With each sunset, a promise reborn,
A tapestry threaded, dreams softly worn,
The horizon beckons, a gentle call,
To rise like the dawn, to break every fall.

In stillness, the soul seeks its way,
Through shadows that dance, where night meets day,
An echo of laughter, a tear that gleams,
Among the horizons, lie woven dreams.

As twilight whispers, secrets unfold,
The beauty of stories yet to be told,
With rays of the moon, guiding our flight,
Into the embrace of the soft starlight.

Liquid Light Dripping from the Soul's Palette

Each stroke a whisper, colors collide,
In a heart's canvas, emotions abide,
Liquid light flows, from essence poured,
Creating beauty, forever adored.

Through vibrant shades, the spirit will dance,
Gifted in visions, the heart's wild chance,
A spectrum of feelings, none left untraced,
Captured in moments, we've softly faced.

Textures of laughter, and tears that glide,
Unraveled stories, too close to hide,
Each heartbeat echoes, a painter's delight,
As the soul spills forth, in radiant night.

In every hue, a journey unfolds,
Writing our truths, in paints of gold,
From dusk till dawn, our spirits ignite,
Together we shimmer, in liquid light.

An Odyssey Beyond the Veils of Perception

Veils of mist, where the senses blur,
Secrets lie deep in the mind's soft purr,
Journeys embark on the wings of the night,
Beyond horizons, where shadows take flight.

A labyrinth woven, with threads of fate,
Paths intertwine, as we contemplate,
In whispers of wisdom, truths come to be,
An odyssey crafted, to set the soul free.

Through windows of wonder, visions arise,
Illuminating fears, with stars in our eyes,
In the quest for meaning, the heart learns to see,
Beyond all illusions, we seek to be free.

This dance of existence, a cosmic embrace,
In every heartbeat, we find our place,
Veils gently lifting, as worlds intertwine,
In this odyssey, forever we shine.

Moonlit Musings of the Soul

Beneath the silver glow of night,
Whispers stir the quiet air,
Hearts unfurl in dream's delight,
As shadows waltz without a care.

Thoughts like stars in endless skies,
Kissed by moonlight's tender grace,
In this stillness, truth complies,
As secrets find their resting place.

Echoes dance in amber beams,
Silent stories softly weave,
In the solace of our dreams,
Our souls' reflections gently believe.

Awakening to dawn's warm light,
The musings fade with morning's call,
Yet in the heart, a spark so bright,
Holds the magic of the fall.

Threads of Delight in the Quiet Hours

In the stillness, whispers weave,
Threads of joy in golden tones,
Quiet moments we perceive,
As laughter softly finds its home.

Gentle breezes brush the trees,
Carrying tales from far and wide,
Their melodies put hearts at ease,
In this calm, our dreams abide.

Mornings painted with soft hues,
Sparkle with the light of grace,
Every moment offers cues,
To find wonder in this space.

As night unfolds its velvet hue,
Stars awaken, bright and bold,
In the quiet, hope renews,
Stories of delight unfold.

The Lightness of Wandering Thoughts

Thoughts that drift like puffs of air,
Float on breezes, light and free,
In this moment, we lay bare,
The depths of our own reverie.

Through the garden of the mind,
Petals fall, oh, so divine,
With each step, new paths we find,
In the dance of space and time.

Chasing clouds that softly pass,
Gathering dreams from sky to ground,
In the stillness, let them last,
Where laughter's echoes can be found.

As the sun begins to set,
Wandering thoughts embrace the night,
In this calm, we won't forget,
The lightness of our hearts in flight.

Dreamscapes Painted in Softest Hues

In the canvas of the night,
Dreams are brushed with pastel shades,
Whispers soft as feathered light,
Guide us through the gentle glades.

Every star a splash of hope,
Draped in twilight's sweet caress,
In this realm, we lovingly elope,
Wandering through the conscious mess.

Imagined worlds begin to bloom,
Petals of color flirt with air,
In this magic, fears consume,
And worries fade beyond compare.

Awakening to morning's grace,
Dreamscapes linger, soft and bright,
In our hearts, they find a place,
Painting joy in every light.

Spirals of Laughter in the Twilight

In twilight's embrace, laughter swirls,
With echoes of joy, the heart unfurls.
Whispers of secrets, in shadows they play,
A dance of the night, where dreams drift away.

Stars gather round, to hear the delight,
Shared moments flicker, like stars in the night.
Laughter ascending, in spirals it flies,
Touching the heavens, beneath painted skies.

Soft breezes carry the tales of our glee,
The world wraps us close, just you and me.
Time pauses gently, in this fleeting space,
Where laughter and twilight share a warm embrace.

Enchanted Echoes of Yesterday

In the silence of dusk, echoes remain,
Whispers of laughter, memories in grain.
Softly they linger, through shadows they wind,
Enchanted reflections, in the heart's mind.

Each moment we cherished, a treasure regained,
Time's gentle fingers, the past unchained.
Woven in silence, the stories unfold,
Enchanted echoes, a tapestry told.

Faces and voices, a magical spell,
In the depths of our hearts, where memories dwell.
Hold me in twilight, let shadows not roam,
Finding enchantment, in whispers of home.

Melodies in the Heart's Attic

In the heart's attic, where memories hum,
Melodies linger, a soft, gentle drum.
Notes of the past flit like dust in the air,
Wrapping around us, a comfort to share.

Each chord a reminder of laughter and tears,
Echoing softly through lingering years.
We climb up the stairs, in search of the tune,
In whispers of sunlight, a song 'neath the moon.

Harmonies healing, our spirits entwined,
As music and moments, in time, we find.
Let these sweet melodies guide us each day,
In the heart's hidden attic, where love has its way.

Kaleidoscope Dreams in Sunbeams

In sunbeams that dance, we chase after light,
Kaleidoscope dreams take vibrant flight.
Colors cascading, in laughter they stream,
Painting the moments, like a sweet dream.

Each turn of the prism, a story to tell,
Bright hues of joy, in which we dwell.
With every heartbeat, we're weaving the bright,
Kaleidoscope visions, a feast for the sight.

Sway with the rhythm, let worries drift free,
In this vivid embrace, just you and me.
Our laughter ignites, in the glow of the sun,
Kaleidoscope dreams, forever we run.

The Tranquil Waltz of Enchanted Hours

In whispers soft, the shadows sway,
Time dances lightly, night turns to day.
Moonlight spills on silken streams,
Where laughter weaves the fabric of dreams.

Stars twinkle like eyes of a friend,
Guiding hearts where enchantments blend.
Every moment feels like a song,
As we waltz through worlds where we belong.

Dreams Flowing Like a River of Light

Gentle currents pull me away,
Into visions where I long to stay.
Each ripple carries a story untold,
In the embrace of dreams, I behold.

The shorelines shimmer with hope anew,
Casting shadows where memories brew.
With every heartbeat, the waters gleam,
As my spirit dances within the dream.

Sunrise Serenade for the Mind's Eye

Awakening hues in the morning's glow,
A canvas painted in soft, warm flow.
Birds sing sweetly to welcome the dawn,
While the world stirs awake, refreshed and reborn.

Golden rays spill through branches wide,
Illuminating paths where dreams abide.
Each note of nature a gentle caress,
Embracing the light, I feel the bliss.

The Art of Floating in a Daydream

Suspended in air, I drift so free,
Caught in the threads of fantasy.
Colors swirl in a splendid dance,
As I lose myself in a trance.

Time slips away like sand through my hands,
Creating worlds where magic expands.
In this realm, my worries cease,
For the art of dreaming brings me peace.

Fleeting Moments in a Timeless Dance

In twilight's glow, we find our place,
Where shadows sway with gentle grace.
Each heartbeat sings, a step, a glance,
Caught in the charm of this sweet dance.

Moments shimmer, like stars they gleam,
Fleeting whispers of a shared dream.
The music plays, we lose all sense,
Bound by time in this sacred suspense.

With every turn, we spin and twirl,
Lost in the magic of a twinkling whirl.
The moment fades, yet we hold tight,
To memories woven in the night.

In this ballet of life, we play,
Where fleeting moments never stray.
A timeless dance, both near and far,
Guided by love, our shining star.

The Rhythms of Laughter Fluttering Free

In fields of gold, laughter rings,
Joy spills forth on vibrant wings.
Children chase as the sun dips low,
In laughter's embrace, we let it flow.

Every giggle, a spark ignites,
Brightening days with pure delights.
Like butterflies, our spirits soar,
In the rhythms of laughter, we explore.

Echoes dance in the soft night air,
Whispers of joy that linger there.
With each shared smile, the world feels right,
Laughter's warm glow, a guiding light.

Together we stand, hearts interlace,
In this symphony, we find our place.
The rhythms of laughter, wild and free,
A timeless bond, in harmony.

Whispers of the Mind's Reverie

In quiet corners of the mind,
Whispers of dreams are softly lined.
Thoughts entwine like vines in bloom,
Painting pictures that chase the gloom.

A gentle breeze, a fleeting thought,
Moments of peace, easily sought.
Imagination soars, breaks the chain,
In reverie, we lose the pain.

Stories weave in shades of night,
Guiding souls to newfound light.
In this haven, we drift and wander,
Exploring the depths, pondering yonder.

Whispers echo in silence deep,
Cradling secrets that we keep.
In the mind's embrace, we truly see,
The beauty of dreams that set us free.

Melodies of a Serene Dreamscape

In a tranquil world, soft notes arise,
Melodies born beneath starlit skies.
Each whispering breeze carries the tune,
Dancing gently, like flowers in bloom.

Rippling rivers hum a sweet refrain,
Echoing peace through the whispering grain.
With every heartbeat, a song takes flight,
Guiding our souls into the night.

In dreamscapes vast, our spirits roam,
Finding solace, a place called home.
Harmony flows like a gentle stream,
Awakening hope, a timeless dream.

The night unfolds, a symphonic blend,
In this serene world where dreams transcend.
Melodies weave through heart and mind,
In the dance of dreams, freedom we find.

Dancing on the Edges of Elysium

In whispers soft as silken night,
We twirl beneath the stars so bright.
With hearts ablaze, we dare to dream,
As moonlight casts its gentle beam.

Each step a spark, a fleeting chance,
In shadows deep, we find our dance.
With every breath, the world we greet,
In rhythm's grace, our souls repeat.

The air alive with laughter's sound,
In this embrace, our hearts are bound.
We chase the dawn, no fear, no pain,
In joy and love, we shall remain.

So let us sway, let worries fade,
On edges where our hopes are laid.
In Elysium's light, we'll forever soar,
Dancing together, forevermore.

Capturing Mirage in a Heartbeat

A fleeting glance, a moment's grace,
In reflections found, I see your face.
Like colors drawn from desert sands,
A mirage born in time's soft hands.

With every sigh, the world does pause,
In the silence, we find our cause.
For heartbeats echo, soft and true,
In this illusion, I'm lost in you.

As daylight fades, and shadows creep,
In twilight's glow, our secrets seep.
We chase the dreams that float away,
In each heartbeat, love finds its way.

So let me hold this fragile spark,
And in your eyes, light up the dark.
For in a heartbeat, all is clear,
This captured mirage, forever dear.

Radiant Echoes of Bliss

In the dawn's embrace, where silence sings,
Radiant echoes of joy take wing.
With every laugh, the world ignites,
A symphony of pure delights.

In fields of gold, where daisies sway,
We dance beneath the bright, warm rays.
With hearts entwined and spirits free,
In moments shared, infinity.

The colors blend, from dusk to dawn,
In twilight's arms, we carry on.
With every heartbeat, life unfolds,
In vibrant hues of crimson golds.

So let the echoes linger long,
In every note, we write our song.
For in this bliss, we find our way,
To weave our dreams into the day.

The Journey Through Twilight's Door

As twilight falls, shadows extend,
We wander paths where dreams ascend.
Each step a story, each sigh a clue,
In dusk's embrace, we find what's true.

The stars awake, a wondrous sight,
Guiding our hearts through the velvet night.
In whispers soft, the secrets flow,
As time reveals what we long to know.

Through painted skies, we chase the light,
In every whisper, in every fight.
With hope as our compass, love our guide,
Together we'll soar, forever side by side.

So let us journey, hand in hand,
Through twilight's door to a promised land.
For in the night, we'll find our way,
A brighter dawn awaits the day.

Behind Closed Eyes: A World Unfurled

In shadows where whispers softly play,
A garden blooms in shades of the gray.
Time lingers still, a soft embrace,
Dreams weave their threads in quiet space.

A river flows in endless streams,
Carrying hopes and fleeting dreams.
Mountains rise with silent grace,
Behind closed eyes, a sacred place.

The sky ignites in fiery hues,
Painting hopes in twilight's views.
Stars emerge, a gentle gleam,
Awakening the slumbering dream.

With every heartbeat, worlds collide,
Within the mind, where secrets hide.
Unfurled and vast, like starlit skies,
Infinite wonders behind closed eyes.

Celestial Patterns Drifted by the Wind

Glimmers of light on the ocean's face,
Dance like whispers, a timeless trace.
Constellations spin in a cosmic waltz,
Guiding our dreams with softest faults.

The wind carries stories from afar,
Brushing the earth with a silver star.
Patterns of fate on the night's embrace,
Celestial paths in a timeless race.

Each breath a bond with the universe,
Drawing in stardust, a whispered verse.
Clouds float gently, crafting a scene,
In the tapestry where we have been.

So close your eyes, let your spirit soar,
Feel the cosmos, forevermore.
In the gentle wind, let the patterns blend,
As celestial stories have no end.

The Symphony of Solitude and Serenity

In quiet corners, where silence hums,
A gentle peace, the heart succumbs.
Notes of stillness, like falling rain,
Compose the air, a soothing strain.

Whispers of nature in swaying trees,
Calmness wrapped in a soft breeze.
The world slows down, a tranquil sigh,
Underneath the vast, open sky.

Each breath a pause, each moment pure,
Echoing thoughts that softly lure.
In solitude's arms, we find our way,
As serenity guides the heart to stay.

This symphony plays, sweet and light,
A melody found in the heart's delight.
In silence and space, we weave our song,
In solitude's grace, we truly belong.

Charms of a Daydreaming Heart

A heart adrift on a cloud of thought,
Where dreams are sown with love, and caught.
Each fluttered wish, a whispered plea,
In the realms of thought, we wander free.

Moments linger like petals in bloom,
Painting the air with sweet perfume.
Visions of joy, like butterflies,
Dance in the light of endless skies.

Through winding paths of ember glow,
Our minds can soar where wishes flow.
Captured in time, forever young,
In daydreams sweet, our hearts are sung.

So let us drift, let our spirits glide,
On currents of wonder, in joy we bide.
With every beat, our dreams impart,
The lovely charms of a daydreaming heart.

Reflections in a Crystal Sea

Waves whisper secrets to the shore,
Mirrored depths hold stories untold.
Sunlight dances on the water's face,
Time drifts gently in this tranquil space.

Ripples of dreams, lost in the tide,
Moments captured, heartache bides.
Glimmers of joy, flickering light,
In this crystal sea, everything feels right.

The horizon melts into a golden hue,
Colors bleed and blend, a painter's view.
Life's reflections sway, ebb, and flow,
In the stillness, the truth can grow.

As I gaze into this sapphire deep,
Memories awaken, stirring from sleep.
In nature's embrace, my soul finds peace,
In each wave, my worries cease.

Threads of Emotion Woven in Silence

In the quiet, hearts softly speak,
A tapestry crafted from joy and grief.
Fingers trace lines where shadows blend,
Each thread a memory that won't end.

Silhouettes dance in the dimming light,
Whispers of laughter mixed with goodnight.
Silence holds truth, loud and clear,
In every heartbeat, love's drawing near.

Colors of sorrow and shades of glee,
Intertwined stories of you and me.
Every stitch tells of moments held dear,
In this weave of life, we draw near.

Underneath the stars, we find our way,
In the tapestry, we choose to stay.
Threads of emotion bind us tight,
In the cloak of night, all feels right.

A Tapestry of Hope and Wonder

Stitched with dreams and woven with care,
A canvas alive with colors rare.
Threads of hope stretch across the night,
Each strand a whisper of morning light.

In every fold, a story unfolds,
Adventures await, both brave and bold.
From shadows cast, new visions spark,
An ember of brilliance ignites the dark.

Wonders await in every seam,
A tapestry woven from our dreams.
In its embrace, we find our way,
Guided by stars that light the day.

Each knot and twist, a choice we make,
A tale of lives that cannot break.
This fabric of life, rich as can be,
A treasure of wonder, wild and free.

Luminescent Journey through Inner Landscapes

Beneath the surface, rivers flow,
A journey through shadows, bright and low.
Mountains rise where fears reside,
In the heart's terrain, we must confide.

Each step illuminated by inner light,
Guides us through the depths of night.
Pathways winding, unseen allure,
In the stillness, we feel so sure.

Fields of thought stretch far and wide,
In every corner, dreams abide.
Emerging visions spark the sky,
A luminescent dance as we fly.

Letting go of burdens, we set free,
This inner landscape speaks to me.
In every heartbeat, we uncover,
The beauty within, our truest lover.

Clouds of Emotion Drifting Softly

Whispers of gray beneath the blue,
Floating gently, weaving through.
A tapestry of feelings unfold,
Stories of joy and hearts turned cold.

With each gust, they swirl and sway,
Carrying dreams that drift away.
A fleeting glimpse of what we feel,
In the soft clouds, our hearts reveal.

Light and dark in a dance divine,
Emotions blend like vintage wine.
Fragile as feathers, bold as rain,
Clouds of emotion whisper our pain.

Beneath their shadows, we find reprieve,
In every cloud, a hope we weave.
Drifting softly, the skies embrace,
A canvas of feelings in infinite space.

The Dance of Dreams on Sunlit Canvas

Golden rays painting thoughts of flight,
Dancing dreams come alive in light.
With laughter, colors boldly blend,
On sunlit canvas, hearts transcend.

Swirling whispers in the summer air,
Echoes of wishes without a care.
Each stroke a journey, wild and free,
Imprinting visions on eternity.

As shadows play and moments glide,
In this dance, we no longer hide.
With every heartbeat, dreams ignite,
On this canvas, everything feels right.

Brushes dipped in hope's embrace,
Creating stories in open space.
The dance of dreams, an endless trance,
In sunlight's glow, we take a chance.

Kaleidoscope of Inner Whispers

Fractured light through prisms beam,
Echoing thoughts, like a silent dream.
A tapestry of hues intertwined,
In this kaleidoscope, secrets unwind.

Whispers of truth in colors so bright,
Dancing shadows, a flickering light.
Each fragment reflects a piece of me,
In this mosaic, my soul is free.

Shifting patterns with every phase,
Mirrored moments in a vibrant haze.
Voices of hope blend in the air,
A kaleidoscope of thoughts laid bare.

Through the patterns, we all can see,
The beauty that stems from you and me.
In whispers and colors, we find our way,
A symphony of souls in bright array.

Heartbeats Intertwined with Stars

In the velvet night where dreams convene,
Two heartbeats echo, a love serene.
Beneath the cosmos, destinies meet,
Whispering tales in rhythm and beat.

Stars ignite like fireflies bright,
Dancing softly in the hush of night.
Each pulse a promise, a silent vow,
Intertwined hearts under the starlit brow.

With every heartbeat, the universe sighs,
Galaxies shimmer in your eyes.
In this celestial embrace, we find,
The infinite love of our souls entwined.

Time stands still as we drift afar,
Lost in the magic of each shining star.
Together we weave a celestial thread,
Heartbeats intertwined, where dreams are led.

Touching the Canvas of Yesterday's Dreams

Faded colors whisper soft,
Memories painted in the sky.
Brushstrokes of laughter and loss,
Time's gentle hand, passing by.

Each hue a story to tell,
In the silence, voices blend.
Echoes linger in the air,
Where yesterdays never end.

Through the frame, shadows dance,
Capturing moments, so bright.
In the gallery of my heart,
Dreams awaken from the night.

With every glance, hope revives,
As colors merge, life is seen.
Touching the canvas with grace,
Whispers of what might have been.

The Glow of Longing in the Twilight Hour

As day surrenders to night,
Shadows blend with fading light.
A soft glow kindles the sky,
Yearning whispers, passing high.

Stars awaken, dreams ignite,
Hearts entwined in gentle flight.
In this hour, thoughts wander,
Across horizons, souls ponder.

With every breath, silence speaks,
Hopes reflected in soft creeks.
Moments linger, feeling near,
In twilight's embrace, we steer.

The glow of longing, so sweet,
Guides us where our dreams do meet.
A tapestry rich and deep,
In twilight's arms, we shall keep.

Serenading the Echo of an Unseen Dance

In moonlight's tender embrace,
Shadows sway with hidden grace.
Soft music lingers in the air,
An echo of souls laid bare.

Whispers twirl in gentle night,
Guided by the stars' soft light.
Every sigh a note set free,
In this dance of you and me.

Step by step, hearts align,
In the rhythm, we entwine.
Unseen movements, pure and true,
Serenading the night anew.

With every turn, secrets shared,
In silence, beauty declared.
The unseen dance, a timeless song,
In this moment, we belong.

Whirls of Unspoken Truths in Eternal Twilight

In twilight's embrace, we stand,
Words unspoken, hand in hand.
Truths wrapped tight in the night's cloak,
Hints of laughter, silence spoke.

The air thick with secrets divine,
As shadows weave and twine.
Each heartbeat echoes the past,
In this moment, forever cast.

Colors blend like thoughts untold,
Mysteries in dusk unfold.
Whirls of dreams caught in the breeze,
Time moves gently, hearts at ease.

In eternal twilight we linger,
Unraveling truths with a finger.
In this space between night and day,
Whispers echo, here we stay.

The Fluttering of Unseen Wings

In secret nooks where shadows play,
Whispers of dreams drift gently sway.
A brush of air, a silent sigh,
Unseen wings dance, as moments fly.

Through twilight's glow, a fleeting trace,
Echoes of joy in a hidden space.
Each flicker bright, a tender spark,
Guiding the lost through the dark.

With every beat, a pulse of grace,
Stories unfold in this sacred place.
The softest touch, a loving nudge,
In the hush, a faithful pledge.

So let us dream beneath the stars,
Where hope takes flight, no boundary bars.
In the silence, hear the song,
Of unseen wings, where we belong.

A Symphony of Wishes and Whims

In a world of colors, bright and bold,
A tale of wishes ready to unfold.
With every heartbeat, dreams ignite,
A symphony of magic in the night.

Laughter rings through the vibrant air,
Dancing shadows everywhere.
Softly spoken, the wishes soar,
Carried gently to distant shores.

Each whim a note in the grand refrain,
Merging hopes with joy and pain.
Together they weave a tapestry fine,
In the orchestra of the divine.

So take a breath, let your heart sing,
Join the dance, let your spirit spring.
For in this melody, we find release,
A symphony of love and peace.

Luminous Threads of Hope

In the twilight of a fading day,
Threads of hope begin to sway.
Woven sunbeams in the dusk,
Filling hearts with gentle trust.

Each whisper glows with promise bright,
Guiding souls through the endless night.
A tapestry of dreams entwined,
In every stitch, the heart aligned.

When shadows loom and spirits wane,
These luminous threads bring joy from pain.
A beacon shines in the darkest hour,
Awakening courage, revealing power.

So hold on tight to these threads so dear,
For hope is vibrant, always near.
In every heartbeat, let it flow,
With luminous threads, let love grow.

Chronicles of a Daydreamer's Heart

In the quiet realms of slumber's grace,
A daydreamer's heart finds its place.
Stories weave through the misty air,
Adventures spark with a hopeful flare.

With eyes half-closed, the magic starts,
Wandering paths of hidden arts.
Each thought a journey, wild and free,
Building worlds for hearts to see.

In the glow of dusk, a tale unfolds,
Echoes of wonders yet untold.
As wishes dance in starry streams,
The daydreamer's heart ignites dreams.

So let us wander, let us roam,
In this enchanted space, our home.
For in the chronicles that we write,
Daydreamers shine, forever bright.

The Melody of Wanderlust Whispers

Footsteps echo on a winding road,
A symphony of dreams unfolds,
The world whispers tales untold,
As the heart seeks to explode.

Stars above dance in the night,
Guiding souls with their light,
Every journey a new delight,
Chasing hope with all our might.

Mountains call with vibrant grace,
Oceans roar, an endless space,
Every turn, a new embrace,
Adventure waits, a sweet embrace.

In every breeze, a story sighs,
A canvas painted with the sky,
With open hearts, we learn to fly,
In wanderlust, we amplify.

Tides of Joy on a Gentle Breeze

Gentle waves kiss the golden shore,
Nature sings, a soft encore,
Sunlight glistens, spirits soar,
In this peace, we find our core.

Breeze carries whispers of the sea,
Each moment flows effortlessly,
Where laughter mingles, wild and free,
Joy ignites like flames of glee.

Children play in sandy bliss,
Each wave a chance, a fleeting kiss,
Memory dances in the mist,
In this paradise, nothing's amiss.

Stars emerge as day bids adieu,
A tranquil night for hearts so true,
In the silence, dreams renew,
With tides of joy, we still pursue.

Paradoxes of a Colorful Mind

Thoughts whirl like hues on a canvas wide,
Reality bends where dreams collide,
Lost in colors, where truths reside,
In paradox, we find our guide.

Daylight brings a shadowed view,
Darkness blooms with shades anew,
Each feeling strange yet pure and true,
In the chaos, creativity grew.

Words dance, conflicting yet sweet,
Harmony found in beats discrete,
Life's riddles make our hearts repeat,
In the vibrance, we dare to meet.

Mind's labyrinth, a vivid sprawl,
Embrace the colors; let them call,
In paradox, we rise, we fall,
Each step revealed, we reconcile all.

Reflections in the Glass of Imagination

Mirrors shimmer with visions bright,
A universe born from sheer delight,
Every thought a spark of light,
In the realm where dreams take flight.

Colors blend in endless streams,
Wonders dance on fleeting beams,
Painting worlds that bend our themes,
In the mind, reality teems.

Whispers echo in the quiet space,
Where shadows twist and visions trace,
Imagining time and endless grace,
In reflections, we find our place.

Shattered glass reveals the soul,
Fragments shimmering, making whole,
In imagination, we play our roles,
In each thought, we grasp our goals.

Colorful Reveries in the Garden of Thought

In the garden where colors bloom,
Dreams weave in a fragrant loom.
Whispers dance on petals bright,
Echoes of joy in morning light.

Glistening dewdrops catch the sun,
Each moment shared is a cherished one.
Butterflies flutter, a soft parade,
In this vibrant world, memories are made.

Gentle breezes sing a sweet tune,
Beneath the gaze of a watchful moon.
Thoughts take root in the fertile ground,
In this garden of wonder, peace is found.

Colorful dreams paint the sky,
As the heart learns to soar and fly.
Among the blooms, hope takes its breath,
In the silence, we discover life's depth.

Embracing the Twilight of Imagination

As shadows stretch and daylight fades,
A canvas of dreams in twilight cascades.
Thoughts like stars, they begin to twinkle,
In the silence, our fears start to crinkle.

Colors merge in a soft embrace,
Time slows down in this mystical space.
Ideas bloom like flowers at dusk,
In the fading light, awakens the husk.

Visions dance like fireflies bright,
Chasing the echoes of the night.
In this hour, magic comes alive,
In the twilight, our dreams will thrive.

With each breath, we weave our tale,
In the stillness, our spirits sail.
Through the darkness, we find our skin,
In the twilight's glow, our journey begins.

When Wishes Take Flight on Silver Wings

Beneath the moon's soft, silver glow,
Wishes flutter, eager to flow.
Carried aloft on whispered dreams,
They glide through night's shimmered beams.

Hearts ignite with hopes untold,
In the stillness, our dreams unfold.
Each desire finds its destined path,
Carving joy from the aftermath.

With every heartbeat, a promise sings,
When wishes take flight on silver wings.
In the quiet, the longing stirs,
As the universe dances, and fate concurs.

Embrace the night, let your spirit soar,
In the embrace of dreams, we're forevermore.
With wishes as stars, and hopes that gleam,
Together we weave the fabric of dream.

A Symphony of Thoughts Beneath the Moon

Notes flutter softly in the night air,
A symphony of thoughts, tender and rare.
Beneath the moon's watchful gaze,
Silent whispers of love and praise.

Melodies dance on cool evening breeze,
In the hush, the heart finds ease.
Reflections shimmer on the surface of time,
In each heartbeat, a rhythm, a rhyme.

Stars join in with their twinkling lights,
Guiding our souls to wondrous heights.
In this serenade, we find our song,
As the moon hums the night along.

Let the music linger, deep and profound,
In the silence, our spirits are found.
With soft harmonies, we take a flight,
In the symphony of thoughts, we unite.

Blossoms of Intention in an Ethereal Breeze

In the garden where dreams reside,
Petals whisper secrets untold,
Each breath of wind, a guiding tide,
Carrying hopes, both fragile and bold.

Glimmers of dawn brush the petals light,
Awakening colors, soft and pure,
Intentions dance in morning's bite,
Nature's embrace, a silent lure.

With every bloom, a story sways,
Fragrant echoes of love's design,
In the sunshine, where laughter plays,
Promises bloom, like sacred wine.

As twilight falls, shadows entwine,
Stars emerge in the velvet night,
The blossoms fade, a sign divine,
In every heart, there dwells the light.

Silken Paths of Memory and Fantasy

Along the lanes where dreams once tread,
Silken whispers brush the air,
Each step retraced, a thread weaved,
In the tapestry of time laid bare.

Memories glimmer, soft and bright,
Like childhood laughter, sweet and clear,
In fantasies, we take to flight,
Chasing shadows, holding dear.

Through golden fields of swaying grass,
The echoes of the past will call,
In fleeting moments, hours pass,
While whispers linger, never small.

Yet in the night, the stars respond,
Painting dreams on the canvas sky,
With memories' touch, our hearts correspond,
In this realm, we learn to fly.

A Canvas Splashed with the Colors of Heart

With every stroke, emotions flow,
On canvas wide, our passions share,
Swirls of joy and shades of woe,
The vivid dance of love laid bare.

Crimson reds and tawny golds,
Blend in harmony, both bright and deep,
A tale of longing, yet untold,
In colors bold, our spirits leap.

Textures rise, where fingers trace,
The story of a life once known,
In this vivid and sacred space,
Our heart's desires, forever shown.

Each painting breathes, a living song,
In hues of dreams, we share our part,
Together bound, where we belong,
On this canvas, the colors of heart.

Transitory Moments at the Edge of Reality

In fleeting hours, where time does sway,
Moments linger, soft as breath,
Between what's real and dreams at play,
Exists a space that feels like death.

A heartbeat quickens, shadows cast,
As whispers of the future blend,
In fragile threads, the present lasts,
Each second holds a chance to mend.

Fragrant echoes of days gone by,
Dance lightly at the edge of night,
In this twilight, we dare to try,
To hold the light and chase the fright.

Yet as dawn breaks, we let it flow,
The moments fade, as dreams take flight,
At the edge of what we know,
We find our strength, we find our light.

Crystalline Drops of Luminal Delight

In the morning light they play,
Drops of dew on petals lay.
Sparkling like the stars above,
Nature's whispers of pure love.

Each shimmer tells a tale untold,
A glimmer of both brave and bold.
They catch the sun and dance so free,
In a world of joy, we find the key.

From blossoms bright to grasses green,
A wondrous sight, a fleeting sheen.
They fade away as time does pass,
But linger still like memories vast.

Crystalline beauty fades from sight,
Yet lingers on in hearts so bright.
A fleeting moment, pure delight,
Captured in love's gentle light.

Dreamcraft Under the Glistening Stars

Beneath the sky, we weave our tales,
With moonlit dreams on silver trails.
Each twinkle is a wish we share,
In whispered hopes, we find our air.

The night unfolds a velvet cloak,
As starlight dances, hearts provoke.
We chase the constellations high,
Embracing moments as they fly.

In cosmic seas, we lose all fears,
With every breath, we shed our tears.
Dreamcraft spins through endless time,
In harmony, we start to climb.

Together, we paint skies of gold,
In this dream space, brave and bold.
Under stars, our spirits soar,
Creating worlds forevermore.

Movements in Time: The Dance of Before and After

In shadows cast by moments past,
The dance of time is flowing fast.
A waltz of whispers, soft and low,
Guiding us where memories glow.

Each step we take, a path we trace,
With echoes of a forgotten place.
Before and after intertwine,
In every heartbeat, every line.

We twirl through ages, lost in thought,
Finding peace in lessons taught.
The present holds both joy and pain,
A tapestry of loss and gain.

And as we spin through space and time,
We discover rhythm, pure and prime.
A dance with fate, a fleeting chance,
To weave our stories in life's dance.

Flight of the Muse in Uncharted Realms

Upon the wings of dreams, we rise,
Exploring worlds that touch the skies.
The muse awakens, guides us near,
To realms unknown, where all is clear.

In uncharted lands, our spirits soar,
With every brush, we yearn for more.
Colors burst in vivid streams,
As we chase down our greatest dreams.

Thought becomes a vibrant hue,
Each note a spark, each word anew.
We dance with shadows, play with light,
In the heart of creation's flight.

With every stroke, we redefine,
The boundaries set by space and time.
In this vastness, we find relief,
The flight of muse, a sweet belief.

The Sweet Lilt of Twilight's Promise

Whispers of dusk touch the sky,
Colors blend as day bids goodbye.
Stars awaken with gentle glow,
Embracing the night, soft and slow.

Dreams begin to weave and dance,
In the twilight's sacred trance.
Hope lingers on the edge of light,
As the world surrenders to night.

Echoes of laughter drift afar,
Fading softly, like a star.
In calmness, secrets start to bloom,
Beneath the soft, enchanting gloom.

The heart finds solace in the shade,
In twilight's veil, fears start to fade.
Sighs mingle with the evening's air,
In this moment, we shed our care.

Tracing the Silhouette of a Hidden Dream

In the silence, shadows play,
Fleeting wonders lost in sway.
Whispers echo through the night,
Guiding thoughts to take their flight.

Figures dance on memory's wall,
Stories waiting for their call.
Each contour speaks of hopes untold,
In the dark, the heart turns bold.

With patience, visions start to form,
In the quiet, thoughts keep warm.
Like delicate sparks against the gloom,
Dreams take shape, begin to bloom.

As dawn approaches, light will break,
Awakening, the soul won't shake.
But still, we hold the dreams we find,
Tracing shadows, heart intertwined.

Ventures along the Veins of Wonder

Paths of curiosity unfold,
Stories of adventure told.
With every step, the heart expands,
In the weave of time, we take our stands.

Mysteries beckon, calling near,
Encasing all that we hold dear.
In the echoes of the wild unknown,
Seeds of bravery have been sown.

Through the forests, under stars,
Finding magic, healing scars.
Each moment crafted with intent,
In the journey, we find content.

As the compass guides our way,
We uncover worlds at play.
In every heart, a light ignites,
Ventures born from starlit nights.

Tides of Reflection on the Sea of Thought

Waves crash softly on the shore,
Whispers of wisdom, ancient lore.
In the stillness, we find our place,
As thoughts drift like clouds in space.

Ripples stretch across the sea,
Carrying secrets, wild and free.
Each moment a glimpse, a chance to see,
What it means to simply be.

In the ebb and flow, we learn to trust,
Immersed in waves of hope and dust.
The depths echo with our fears,
Yet we rise, releasing tears.

As dawn breaks, colors ignite,
Reflecting dreams in morning's light.
We sail upon the tides of grace,
Finding solace in this space.

The Fable of Unspoken Emotions

In shadowed corners, whispers dwell,
Words unsaid begin to swell.
Hearts entwined yet still apart,
Muffled echoes, a silent art.

The gaze lingers, but lips stay closed,
A tale of longing, softly proposed.
In dreams we speak, without a sound,
Love's language lost, yet still profound.

Through moments fleeting, glances meet,
A tapestry of tales discreet.
In every sigh, a story lies,
Unshared truths beneath the skies.

Yet still we hope, in starlit nights,
To find a way to share our sights.
For what is life but some refrain,
In silent verses, joy and pain.

Rhapsody in a Morning Mist

The dawn unfolds in silver gray,
As fog wraps secrets in its play.
Gentle whispers brush the trees,
Nature's breath, a soft reprise.

Birds awaken, serenade the light,
Each note dances, a pure delight.
Buds bloom shy, beneath the veil,
In crisp air, sweet stories sail.

Paths emerge from hazy dreams,
Flowing streams and sunlit beams.
A world reborn in tender glow,
Embracing all, both high and low.

As morning shines, the mist will fade,
Unveiling wonders, unafraid.
In every drop, a promise springs,
Rhapsody that morning brings.

Journeys Through a Gossamer World

On gossamer threads, dreams take flight,
Floating softly through the night.
Each step a dance on fragile ground,
In whispered realms, magic's found.

Moonlit paths weave tales anew,
With silken stars, bright and true.
Every heartbeat, a gentle sigh,
As time drifts softly, passing by.

Glimmers of hope through twilight's grace,
A fleeting touch, a warm embrace.
Floating whispers, secrets spun,
In this world, we're all but one.

So take my hand, let's drift away,
In gossamer dreams, we'll find our way.
Where shadows dance and laughter sings,
A journey born on fragile wings.

The Lilt of Anxious Fantasies

In shadows deep, the mind does drift,
Chasing visions, a tremulous gift.
Thoughts like birds in frantic flight,
Anxious dreams that haunt the night.

Each whispered fear, a haunting rhyme,
Pulsing rhythms, out of time.
Chimeras rise where silence reigns,
Echoing doubts, and heart's refrains.

Yet in that lilt, a spark does glow,
In fragile hopes, we learn to grow.
As shadows fade, we seek the light,
Finding strength to face the fright.

So let us weave through tangled thoughts,
Unearth the peace that life has sought.
For in the dream, where spirits soar,
We find our voice, forevermore.

Twinkling Glimmers of Enchanted Reveries

In whispers soft like evening's glow,
Dreams dance lightly in the flow.
Stars above in twilight beams,
Hold the secrets of our dreams.

With laughter faint and shadows cast,
Moments linger, blinking fast.
Time becomes a gentle sigh,
As night unveils the velvet sky.

In corners where the wild winds sing,
We find the magic memories bring.
Through the threads of stardust spun,
We chase the night, and greet the sun.

Thus twinkling glimmers softly weave,
A tapestry we dare believe.
In echoes soft, our hearts expand,
With enchanted dreams, forever stand.

The Serendipity of Touching Clouds

Drifting high where whispers meet,
Softened edges, light and sweet.
Floating dreams on silken air,
A gentle touch, a moment rare.

In cotton fields, the sun will play,
As we lose ourselves, come what may.
Wings unfurl with every sigh,
In this world, we learn to fly.

Above the noise, a peaceful dome,
Wrapped in warmth, we find our home.
Beneath the heavens, hearts unfold,
In serendipity, stories told.

With fingers tracing paths unknown,
We harvest dreams, our seeds are sown.
In clouds, we find the magic flow,
A dance of fate, where wishes grow.

Pastel Skies of Forgotten Longings

Beneath the hues of dawn's embrace,
Whispers of time a subtle trace.
Fleeting thoughts in lavender light,
Recall the echoes of the night.

Brush strokes soft on canvas gray,
Paint the dreams that drift away.
In muted tones, our hearts reside,
Where lost desires gently hide.

Each pastel shade, a promise worn,
Of wishes dreamed and hearts reborn.
Through twilight's veil, our shadows blend,
In longing's grasp, we seek to mend.

Yet in the softness, hope appears,
As colors shift through laughter's tears.
In pastel skies, we find release,
In forgotten longings, there is peace.

Mosaics of Euphoria in Fleeting Glances

In every gaze, a story shines,
A spark of joy, a thread that binds.
Mosaics made of moments bright,
Reflecting all that feels so right.

With every glance, the world unfolds,
In fleeting looks, our hearts are bold.
Between the beats, in silent grace,
We weave a dance, a warm embrace.

Fragments of laughter in the air,
Glimpses shared without a care.
In vivid hues, we find our song,
In fleeting glances, we belong.

Euphoria blooms like wildflowers,
In tiny moments, endless hours.
As life creates its intricate dance,
Through all the beauty, we find our chance.

Milton Keynes UK
Ingram Content Group UK Ltd.
UKHW022008131124
451149UK00013B/1063